Pierre Elliott Trudeau

#15

The prankster who never flinched

Written by Sandra Phinney

Illustrated by Gabriel Morrissette

© 2006 JackFruit Press Ltd.
Publisher — Jacqueline Brown
Editor — Susan Hughes
Series Editor — Helen Waumsley
Designer and Art Director — Marcel Lafleur
Researchers — Barbara Baillargeon and Hagit Hadaya

JackFruit Press Ltd.
Toronto, Canada
www.jackfruitpress.com

Library and Archives Canada Cataloguing in Publication

Phinney, Sandra
Pierre Elliott Trudeau: The prankster who never flinched / written by Sandra Phinney; illustrated by Gabriel Morrissette.

(Canadian prime ministers: warts and all)
Includes index.

ISBN 0-9736406-5-0

1. Trudeau, Pierre Elliott, 1919–2000—Juvenile literature. 2. Prime ministers—Canada—Biography—Juvenile literature. 3. Canada—Politics and government—1968–1979—Juvenile literature. 4. Canada—Politics and government—1980–1984—Juvenile literature. I. Morrissette, Gabriel, 1959-   . II. Title. III. Series.

FC626.T7P49 2006
j971.064'4092   C2006-901647-X

Printed and bound in Canada

This book tells the story of Pierre Trudeau, Canada's 15th prime minister.

When he first came to power, Pierre was considered really cool, a real celebrity . . .

Later on, some people called him a "philosopher king." Others called him all kinds of things we can't print here!

Contents

Hot topics

Pierre Elliott Trudeau:

All of a sudden, Canadian politics aren't dull anymore. Pierre Trudeau doesn't take authority too seriously. He ruffles a lot of feathers by showing up in the House of Commons wearing sandals and corduroy pants. He also does irreverent things like sliding down banisters and pirouetting behind the Queen's back.

A "take it or leave it" leader

Countries have always had leaders . . . some good, some not so good. Once in a while, a country is lucky enough to have a great leader—someone who leaves his or her personal mark on history. Pierre Elliott Trudeau was such a leader. He cared about people's rights and he believed in justice. He believed that people had the right to have more choices about how to lead their lives. And he didn't just talk about these important things (although he was really good at that too!). When he was justice minister, he worked hard to change the laws in Canada so they were fair to everyone. He changed the **criminal code** so that certain actions were no longer illegal. He wanted people to understand that just because they might think an action was wrong or against their religion, it didn't mean it was a crime.

Pierre was always very concerned about young people. When he became prime minister, he developed several special programs for youth, such as **Katimavik** and **Canada World Youth**. Pierre appointed women to important jobs in government. He established the Official Languages Act, which made both English and French the official languages of Canada. When Pierre became prime minister of Canada, Britain still had control over Canada's **constitution**, which is the set of rules that outlines how a country runs. Pierre won the right for Canada to make changes to its own constitution without ever again needing Britain's permission. These were just a few things that he accomplished. Pierre also inspired the people of Canada to believe in themselves and this wonderful country. He made people think and care.

Politically incorrect

But hey! Don't get the idea that this guy was always politically correct. Quite the opposite was true. He once called the **Liberal party** "a herd of donkeys." Sure, that was before he started thinking about becoming a politician. But even still, he was never shy about saying what he thought. And as it turned out, the Liberal party didn't seem to hold his comment against him. They elected him as their party leader in 1968!

He also had a knack for not taking authority too seriously. Take his fashion choices, for example. Early in his career, when he was minister of justice, he ruffled a lot of feathers by wearing a yellow polka-dot ascot to work instead of a tie. He often showed up at work wearing sandals and corduroy pants. Pierre also made some, well, irreverent gestures while he was in political office. He slid down a banister at a serious political conference, and he once pirouetted behind **Queen Elizabeth II**'s back at Buckingham Palace. All of a sudden, Canadian politics weren't dull anymore.

An all-or-nothing guy

Pierre was an all-or-nothing kind of guy. He never went halfway on anything. He thrived on challenges and always pushed himself to the limit. Pierre was fascinated by sports, and he excelled in canoeing, skiing, and hiking. He swam often, climbed mountains, practised yoga, went scuba diving, and had a brown belt in judo.

This intelligent guy had a brain that operated like a computer and a memory that astounded people. Pierre believed that people should debate ideas, not feelings, which is why his motto was "reason over passion." He was also extremely charismatic and charming. He drove fancy sports cars and dated famous actresses, singers, and musicians. Whenever he wore a suit or jacket, he made a personal statement by sporting a red rose in his lapel.

Some people have called Pierre stingy. He was a millionaire (thanks to inheriting some family money and making smart investments), but he rarely left a decent tip in a restaurant and he once fought against an $8 tax increase on his summer home. However, the same man sent $3,000 to a penniless friend living in Paris and, when he practised law, defended many people for free.

Yes, Pierre was a complicated man. He enjoyed playing pranks and had a tendency to show off. But he also had a brilliant mind and a compelling vision for Canada's future.

Want to know more? The words in bold are explained in the glossary at the back of the book.

Pierre thrives on challenges and always pushes himself to the limit. He excels in canoeing, skiing, and hiking. He also swims a lot, climbs mountains, practises yoga, scuba dives, and has a brown belt in judo.

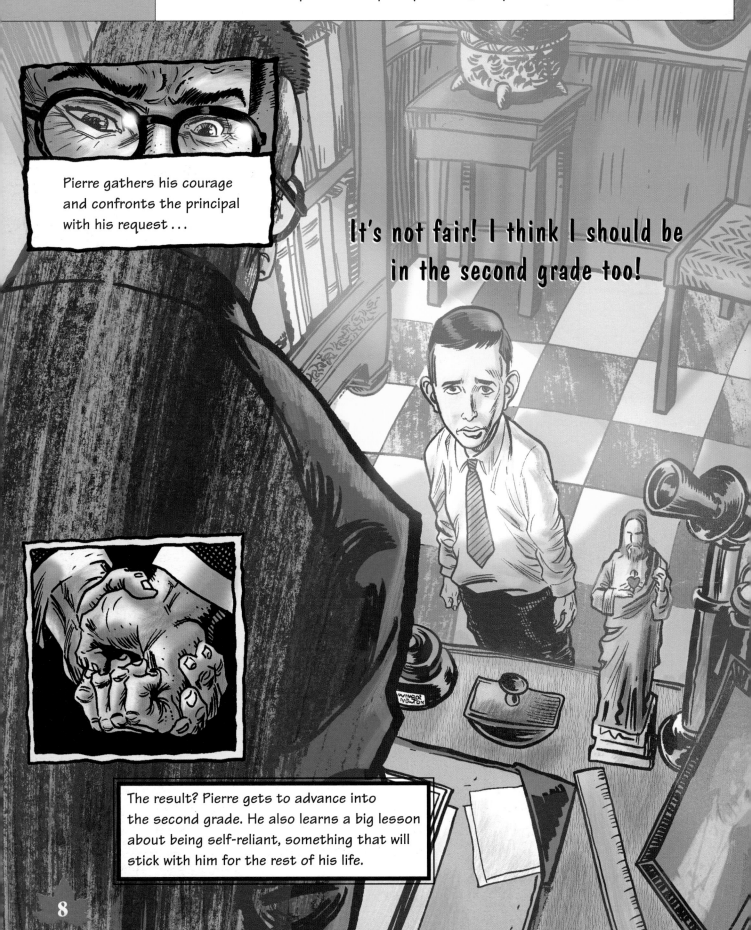

1925

Pierre gets upset when a friend is placed in the second grade just because he's bigger. He complains to his father. "It's not fair. I should be in the second grade too." His dad refuses to speak to the principal. "It's your problem. Ask him yourself."

Pierre gathers his courage and confronts the principal with his request . . .

It's not fair! I think I should be in the second grade too!

The result? Pierre gets to advance into the second grade. He also learns a big lesson about being self-reliant, something that will stick with him for the rest of his life.

Chapter 1
Growing up, speaking up

Joseph Phillipe Pierre Yves Elliott Trudeau came into this world on October 18, 1919. He was the son of **Charles Émile Trudeau**, a French Canadian, and **Grace Elliott**, daughter of a French-Canadian mother and a Scottish father. From the beginning, family and friends called the boy Pierre. For a time, he experimented with his name, trying out Pierre-Phillipe (after his grandfather), and Pierre Esprit (after Pierre Esprit Radisson, the explorer), before settling on Pierre-Elliott Trudeau (combining his French and English heritage). He later dropped the hyphen. The world would come to know him as Pierre Elliott Trudeau.

Assuming everyone else is bilingual

Pierre lived in a small home on Rue Durocher in Montreal. He grew up playing with kids from various religions and backgrounds. He spoke French with his dad and usually English with his mother, and thought that everyone was bilingual.

When he started grade one at Académie Querbes, skinny Pierre was upset that his friend Gerald O'Conner was placed in the second grade just because he was bigger. Pierre complained, "It's not fair. I should be in the second grade too." Pierre's father refused to speak to the principal for him. "It's your problem. Ask him yourself." Pierre was a sensitive, shy child. But he gathered his courage and went to see the principal. The result? Pierre got permission to advance into the second grade. He also learned a big lesson about being self-reliant, something that stuck with him for the rest of his life.

1919
Pierre is born in Montreal on October 18. He has an older sister named Suzette.

1921
His brother, Charles, is born.

1925
Pierre begins primary school in Montreal.

1931
Pierre's father sells his chain of garages for $1,400,000. The family is now rich.

1933
Pierre visits Europe for two months with his family. He discovers a love of travel and other cultures.

1935
Pierre's father dies.

1943
Pierre graduates from the University of Montreal with a law degree.

1944
Pierre hitchhikes across Mexico.

Pierre begins a doctorate degree in political economics.

1946-48
Pierre studies in Paris and London.

1948
Pierre, 29, leaves on a 'round-the-world backpack trip to Poland, Czechoslovakia, Austria, Hungary, Turkey, Israel, Pakistan, and China. From China, Pierre takes a ship to Japan, Hawaii, and San Francisco.

Bet you've heard of hazing—where senior students hassle first-year students.

Well, when a senior student threw a banana in Pierre's soup, Pierre fished it out and threw it back, not realizing that he was not supposed to try to get even with senior students.

The angry student demanded that Pierre meet him after school, where they could "settle it outside."

Pierre was probably shaking in his boots, but he just stood his ground and looked the bully straight in the eye, not saying a word. The bully backed down! Once again, Pierre had not flinched.

Order and freedom

When Pierre was in elementary school, his hard-working father was a lawyer and owned a chain of 30 service stations. Gutsy and boisterous, he hugged people a lot, laughed a lot, and swore a lot. Charles Émile was a short, strong man who enjoyed the outdoors and sports. He taught his son how to box, shoot a rifle, paddle a canoe, and play poker.

Pierre's mother was slender, gentle, and had a soft voice. Her son inherited her beautiful blue eyes. Grace played the piano and taught her three children about music. She took Pierre, his older sister Suzette, and younger brother Charles to concerts and the ballet. She also loved to ski and go for motorbike rides. When he got older, Pierre often said that his father taught him order and discipline and his mother showed him a life of freedom and fantasy.

A sudden change in fortune

When Pierre was 12 years old, his father sold the chain of garages to Imperial Oil for $1.4 million dollars (that would be about $18 million dollars today). All of a sudden the Trudeau family was rich. The family moved from their modest house at the edge of the city to a three-storey home in the posh part of town at the foot of Mount Royal. Now the family chauffeur drove the children to school.

But the most exciting thing for Pierre was a trip to Europe that the family made in the summer of 1933. For two glorious months they travelled to countries like Italy, France, and Germany. Pierre never got tired of going to different places and meeting new people. His father often gave him tasks to do, like going into a hotel to see if there were any rooms or visiting a store to look for rare books. In many places Pierre couldn't speak the language of the country, so it was a big challenge—but he usually succeeded.

Only two years later, Pierre's father died on a trip to Florida with his baseball team, the Montreal Royals. Pierre was only 15 years old at the time and the loss hit him hard.

Charles Émile had enjoyed challenging and debating with Pierre, creating a love of learning in his son. Pierre went to Collège Jean-de-Brébeuf, an elite high school run by **Jesuits** (an order of Roman Catholic priests). He loved his time there even though they had classes six days a week. He learned old languages like ancient Greek and Latin, how to question things, and how to argue effectively. Pierre hated to lose an argument, and he could be a real pain in the neck because he always wanted to have the last word. One of the ways he did this was by answering a question with a question!

The Collège Jean-de-Brébeuf is an elite school run by Jesuits. Pierre loves school and always gets top marks. He even studies lessons that have not yet been assigned. He hangs out with a brainy crowd, known as *les snobs*. He's also quite a prankster.

Pierre and his friends form a group called the Club of the Dying. They turn stiff as a board and topple over, breaking their fall with their hands at the very last second. They pull this prank all over school.

Unlike many other guys his age, Pierre didn't get involved in World War II.

Many French-Canadians refused to get involved in the war. They saw it as a fight that had nothing to do with them.

Joining the army was voluntary, so Pierre opted not to. He continued his university studies instead.

In Quebec, especially, the war was seen only as a battle among foreign superpowers.

Pierre was very competitive and always got top marks. He even studied the sections of the lessons that the teachers didn't assign. He wanted to learn everything he possibly could. He hung out with a brainy crowd, and others referred to them as *les snobs*.

Imagining the future

Later, when Pierre started to think about his future, he imagined everything from being a sea captain to an astronaut. But first he had some exploring to do. He planned an ambitious canoe trip with two cousins in the summer of 1941. They started in Montreal and canoed along an old voyageur route all the way up to James Bay—over 800 kilometres! Then they hitchhiked back to Montreal, sending their canoes home by train.

In 1943, Pierre completed his law degree, graduating with honours from the University of Montreal. He spent a year working for a law firm. Then he went to Mexico City to study Spanish and, once there, ended up hitchhiking across the country. But he couldn't quite give up school yet. He started another degree, this time in economics and political science, at Harvard University, in the United States. Then he did more studying in Paris, France and London, England.

Around the world

Now 29 years old, Pierre was ready for more exploring. In the spring of 1948, he set out with his backpack to journey around the world. It was a big challenge. Could he survive in the Middle East, where people were at war? Or in Turkey or China where he couldn't speak the language? You bet! He had lots of hair-raising experiences. He was put in a Yugoslavian jail for not having a visa, and he got caught in a crossfire in Jerusalem. He even outsmarted some desert bandits in Iraq. When they threatened him, Pierre started screaming poetry at them, yelling out verse after verse, rolling his eyes and making ridiculous gestures with his arms and legs. Thinking he was both insane and dangerous, the bandits took off!

Eventually, after travelling partly by boat through India, Pierre reached China. Many of the things he observed there made him sad. The country was at war. He saw starving troops, citizens being shot dead, and thousands of people trying to leave the country. This fuelled his passion for justice and freedom. Pierre knew it was time to go home.

Pierre wondered what he would find when he finally reached Montreal. As he began to make his way back to Canada, his worries about his home province returned to trouble him. In Quebec, most of the important, well-paying jobs were given to English people. The average working person had no power, very little money, and very little hope for the future. The province was not keeping up with the rest of the world.

How travel abroad expanded Pierre's mind

An old adage says that travel broadens the mind. This is especially true when you travel abroad because it allows you to see how the neighbourhood you grew up in is only one way of seeing things and understanding life.

Pierre was one of those people whose mind was expanded because he was open to what the world had to offer. Both of his parents had prepared him for this early in life. His mother had trained him by taking him on long canoe trips in the Quebec wilderness. This taught Pierre to connect with nature and find his way around unfamiliar surroundings. His dad sharpened his confidence by testing his capacity to deal with foreign clerks in stores, hotels, and restaurants while on an extended holiday in Europe.

As soon as Pierre finished university, he went on a trip around the world carrying only a backpack, his clothes, and a little money. Often travelling on foot, horse, or camel, Pierre trekked across Europe and Asia, where he sometimes found himself in war zones and in real danger. Pierre usually travelled alone. This made it easier for him to go wherever he wanted. It also allowed him to test himself. How would he handle himself in China, not knowing the language or the culture and having nobody to rely on but himself?

One of Pierre's most exciting trips was to Moscow, capital of the Soviet Union. It happened during the middle of the **Cold War**, when tensions and hostility between the Communist and Western worlds were at a peak. Pierre enjoyed his time in Moscow because he was able to see how a lot of Western propaganda about the Soviet people and the communist system simply wasn't true. But his natural curiosity almost landed him in jail. He aroused the suspicion of the Soviet government by wandering around Moscow, talking to ordinary people and asking them their opinions. Because of this, the KGB (Soviet secret-service agents) followed him wherever he went. Pierre knew what they were doing. Prankster that he was, he took time to tease the KGB agents by doing things like throwing a snowball at a statue of the Soviet leader, Joseph Stalin.

As much fun as it was, Pierre's world tour was more than just a series of exciting adventures. It shaped his mind. He saw first-hand how different cultures and political systems succeeded or failed to solve their problems. He observed how some countries rejected old authoritarian ways and became more open. He noticed how ordinary people around the world were beginning to claim and enjoy more personal freedom. Returning home, Pierre could more clearly see how narrow and limited life still was in Quebec. He had always known that big business and religion had a tight grip on Quebec society. He now felt that he knew better how to change what he saw as an old and failing system.

Most of all, Pierre's travels made him appreciate the genius and creativity of other cultures. In turn, this led him to promote tolerance and encourage Canadians to respect each other's rights, celebrate their diverse backgrounds, and build a better future for themselves and Canada.

For more information about travelling abroad, visit our website at www.jackfruitpress.com.

Returning home after travelling around the world, Pierre sees that Quebec is still stuck in the past. Its government is still in cahoots with the Catholic Church. Both resist change, controlling what books people can read and what plays and movies they can watch.

Society has to change to meet the needs of its citizens!

Eager to change things, Pierre joins a reporter friend who's covering a strike by asbestos-mine workers. Noticing how the police use force to break up the strike, Pierre gets involved and works for free on behalf of the miners.

Chapter 2

Pierre takes action

H aving travelled in Canada, the United States, Mexico, Europe, the Middle East, and Asia, Pierre had experienced almost every political system you can think of. For him, every country was a new adventure. Everywhere he went, he asked himself, "What kind of society is better for people? What kind of government suits their needs best? What makes them happier? What system allows individuals the most personal freedom within their laws?"

When he returned home in 1949, Pierre was disappointed to see that nothing had changed in Quebec. The Catholic Church continued to have a lot of power—too much power, Pierre thought. For example, it decided what books people could read and what plays and movies people could watch. And worse, Quebec's provincial government supported the

Church. It too resisted change. The province was not keeping up with the rest of the world.

Pierre now wanted to work for the things he believed in. He wanted to change things. An old friend and newspaper reporter, **Gérard Pelletier**, was writing about the strike of asbestos-mine workers in Quebec. Pierre went with Pelletier to observe the situation. Police were using force to break up the strike. Pierre believed the miners were being treated unfairly. He made speeches and worked for justice on their behalf—for free—until the strike ended in July.

Now, at age 30, Pierre wondered if getting involved in politics might be a way to help bring change to Quebec. To learn more about politics, he got a job that summer in Ottawa as a legal adviser to the **Privy Council Office**, a federal government department. But he got itchy feet. Thinking he would be more useful in Quebec, he returned to Montreal. Pierre and some friends started a magazine, *Cité Libre* (*Free City*). They wrote articles that spoke against the practices of the Church and government. They hoped their words would get people to wake up to what was happening.

A new way to fight

Throughout the 1950s, Pierre practised law, taught basic business skills to union leaders, and continued helping union workers negotiate better deals with their employers. He spoke out against the ways in which the Church and government were misusing their power. Fighting against powerful people and institutions was a brave thing to do—and not without consequences for Pierre. Quebec Premier **Maurice Duplessis** actually blocked Pierre's path three times when he applied to teach at the University of Montreal. But that didn't stop him. He continued to support people and their rights—in his articles, in the courts, and in the classroom.

Many people, called separatists, believed that the only way to improve things in Quebec was for it to separate from Canada and become its own country. Pierre disagreed. He believed Quebecers needed a new provincial government. This would give people choices and more freedom. Quebec could remain part of Canada and still be free to celebrate its own language and unique culture.

By 1960, there was a new provincial government, and some changes did occur. Pierre was even invited to teach at the University of Montreal, and he accepted.

Five years later, he was ready to try a new way to fight for more changes. In the 1965 election, Pierre agreed to run for the Liberal

Pierre would never interrupt an opponent, but when the other person paused, he'd slip in a wisecrack to undercut his rival's argument. It was a habit that stayed with him his whole life.

Appointed as the new minister of justice, Pierre immediately starts loosening Canada's outdated laws on divorce, same-sex relationships, and privacy. But his biggest job is convincing Canadians to agree.

The state has no business in the bedrooms of the nation.

Pierre insists that the government should respect people's privacy and not interfere in their sexual lives. He changes the criminal code to reflect this.

In 1965, union leader <u>Jean Marchand</u> was invited to run as a candidate for the Liberals under Prime Minister Lester Pearson.

Marchand would do so only if his old friends Pierre Trudeau and Gérard Pelletier did the same. He knew that a lone Quebecer would be ignored by the party and in Parliament.

Lester wasn't convinced it was a good idea, but eventually became impressed with the three of them, especially Trudeau. The trio became known around town as the Three Wise Men —or "les trois colombes" (the three doves) in French.

party—the party he'd poked fun at. The young candidate was voted in. Off he went to Ottawa as a **member of Parliament**. Before he knew it, Pierre was invited to be **parliamentary secretary** to Prime Minister **Lester B. Pearson**. Pierre thought he'd be doing "parliamentary chores and some pencil-pushing." He expected his job to be tame—even boring. Instead, he ended up going all over the world on government business. Paris, Lagos, New York! Not tame. Definitely not boring.

Minister of justice

Sixteen months later, the prime minister appointed Pierre as the new minister of justice. He took to it like a duck to water. Right away he started making changes to Canada's criminal code. Many of its laws were outdated. Some laws, for example, made it difficult for people to divorce and made abortion (a surgical way to end pregnancy) illegal. Pierre prepared a new bill to loosen many of these laws. But his biggest job was convincing Canadians to agree to these changes. In 1967, he argued that "the state has no business in the bedrooms of the nation." Pierre changed the laws that said you could be arrested for having a sexual relationship with someone of the same gender. He did this because he believed that the government should respect people's privacy. There were many heated arguments across the country, but the bill that contained the changes became law in 1969.

Meanwhile, Prime Minister Pearson made plans to retire and asked Pierre to run as the party's leader. Pierre worried that he didn't have enough experience. He knew he would be kissing his freedom good-bye. But in spite of his reservations, he decided to run. In 1968, Pierre was elected as the Liberal party's leader and, oh yes, took Pearson's place as the new prime minister of Canada as well.

Canadian families are not what they used to be

Long ago, people married when they were quite young and usually had some kids—sometimes 8, 12, or 15 of them! In those days, adoption was rare. Also, parents hardly ever separated or divorced. The law made it difficult to do, and not many people considered it an option. It was not common for a child to be brought up by a single parent.

When Pierre was minister of justice, he changed the criminal code to make it easier for women to get a divorce. His changes to the law made it possible for people of the same sex to have relationships and live together without breaking the law.

Pierre made these changes to Canadian law because he had been looking at the needs of the people around him. He had noticed that the world was changing and people were living their lives differently from the way their own parents and grandparents had lived. Pierre's goal had been to reflect those changes. And when he did, he helped people become more comfortable about the choices they were already making. Little by little, families kept changing.

Instead of marrying when they're 20 years old, many people now wait until they're in their 20s or 30s. Some people decide not to get married but to live together as a permanent couple. (This is called a common-law relationship.) Married or not, people are continuing to have children. Some have many children. Others—more and more—have only one or two. Some families choose not to have any children.

According to the 2001 Statistics Canada census, there were 8.4 million families in Canada that year.

The official definition of "family" includes married couples and common-law couples—of the same or opposite sex—with or without children. Families also include single parents, like Pierre Trudeau was, living with their children. In recent years, same-sex couples have been allowed to adopt children and raise their own families. Families are raising children that are born to them, foster children, or adopted children. Did you know that there are almost 5,000 adoptions every year in Canada? We also have thousands of foster families.

As Canadian society has continued to change, the whole idea of family has continued to evolve. Many families now extend beyond bloodlines. For example, people who work together often feel as if their coworkers are family. This is especially true of soldiers, airforce pilots, and firefighters.

Some families come together after a major disaster or some other important event that changes everyone's life in a big way. In the aftermath of Hurricane Katrina, many homeless people were adopted by church groups, local organizations, or even ordinary families who gave them shelter and support. In such cases, those needing help and those giving it bonded in ways similar to a family, and even began to think of themselves as such.

Other families are made up of people who choose to take care of each other because they share a common cause. Such chosen families might include homeless street kids or other individuals who share a common problem or outlook.

What used to be a fixed idea of family is now adapting and becoming even broader as our society faces new changes and challenges.

For more information about Canadian families, visit our website at www.jackfruitpress.com.

1968

On the night before his election, Pierre is in Montreal, sitting on an outdoor balcony with some other dignitaries. He's watching a parade that takes place every year on Quebec's St-Jean-Baptiste Day.

You leave if you want to. I'm not going to be bullied. I'm staying right here!

Some people are throwing bottles and rocks at the balcony. Everyone on the balcony flees—except Pierre. He defiantly keeps his seat and continues watching the parade. His unspoken message to the protesters is loud and clear: "You can't bully me." His courage pays off. Next day at the polls, the Liberal party wins more than half of the 264 seats in the House of Commons.

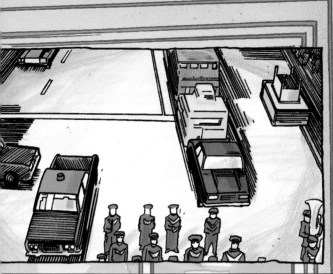

The parade is going along smoothly when bottles suddenly start to whiz by Trudeau and other dignitaries on the balcony.

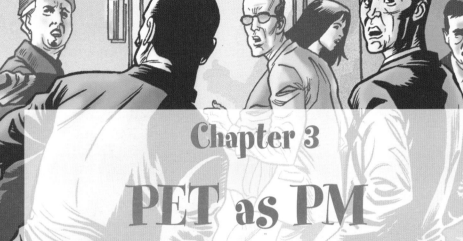

Chapter 3

PET as PM

Pierre was 49 years old and unmarried. It must have been strange for him to move into the big house overlooking the Ottawa River. This was **24 Sussex Drive**, the official residence of every prime minister of Canada since 1955. Pierre arrived at his new digs with only two suitcases. At the time, he didn't know if he would be there for a few months or several years. He had a choice to make. If he chose to stay on as prime minister and ride out the remaining 18 months of Pearson's term, he could. Or he could call an election and try to get elected on his own steam. If he were successful, he'd have that position for at least four years.

Guess what he did? This self-confident fellow figured that he had a good chance of getting elected. By now, Pierre was used to setting up interesting challenges and figuring out what to do. And remember—once he set his mind on winning something, nothing could stop him. So on April 23, 1968, just three days after he took over the reins of the Liberal party, he surprised everyone by calling an election for June 25.

1968

Pierre replaces Lester B. Pearson as leader of the Liberal party.

Pierre is elected prime minister. The Liberals win with a majority.

Lincoln MacCauley Alexander becomes the first black member of Parliament.

René Lévesque founds the separatist Parti Québécois.

US civil rights leader Martin Luther King is assassinated.

1969

The Official Languages Act orders that all federal services be available in French and English.

New Brunswick becomes first province to be officially bilingual.

Results of the 1968 election:

Pierre Elliott Trudeau becomes Canada's 15th prime minister

Population:	20,014,880	
Eligible voters:	10,860,888	
Valid votes cast:	8,125,996	

How the numbers stacked up:

Party	# votes	# seats
PC	2,554,880	72
Liberal	3,696,945	155
NDP	1,378,260	22
Other	495,911	15
Total	8,125,996	264

Issues: Quebec separation

Pierre liked to play tricks on the press. Reporters knew that Pierre might not tell them in advance that he was calling an election, and they wanted to be the first to know! They knew that when a prime minister wants to call an election, he has to get permission from the **governor general**. So they staged a watch on the front lawn of Sussex Drive so that they could track the prime minister's movements. It didn't work. On April 23, Pierre sneaked out of his office by a hidden staircase, slipped over to the governor general's home, and entered by a side gate. The media only learned of his decision later, when he announced it in the **House of Commons** that afternoon.

Dreaming of a just society

Now Pierre really got down to work. He had only two months to convince Canadians that he was the right person to lead the country. His campaign focused on his dream that Canada would be a just society. He believed it could be "a humane, caring, freedom-loving society of many peoples, traditions, and beliefs." As he travelled across the country to speak to Canadians, thousands came out to listen to his speeches. Crowds treated Pierre like a famous rock star or sports hero. Women wanted to kiss him, and some went hysterical when they saw him. The country seemed to fall in love with Pierre. Trudeaumania was born.

But Trudeaumania was much more than Pierre himself. It was a mix of joy, hope, and mass giddiness that took over the country during Expo '67, which put Canada on the world map, and Canada's 100th birthday celebrations.

Canadians were feeling mighty good about themselves, their country, and their future. Pierre became the focal point for the dream of a better society run by a younger generation.

Of course, some Canadians didn't like Pierre or his ideas, including his belief that Quebec should not separate from Canada. On June 24, the night before the election, Pierre was in Montreal watching a parade that takes place every year on Quebec's national holiday, St-Jean-Baptiste Day (now known as Fête nationale du Québec). He was sitting on an outdoor balcony with some other dignitaries. Suddenly things started to whiz by his head. A group of separatists was throwing bottles and rocks at him. Everyone fled—except Pierre. He defiantly kept his seat and continued watching the parade. His unspoken message to the agitators was loud and clear: "You can't bully me." Next day at the

What would a just society actually be like?

Pierre Trudeau was a man who liked to think about big ideas. When he went to school, he'd spend his time reading all the great philosophers and thinkers. They made him think about what kind of country and world he wanted to live in, and how he could make it better. As he went through school and became active in politics, his own ideas grew. One of these ideas was that Canada needed to try harder to become a "just society."

What would a just society be like? It's a tough question, actually; everyone has their own ideas about what it would look like. Religion, culture, history, and other factors would all play a role. Pierre himself believed that a just society needed at least two things: freedom and equality. But what about justice, liberty, or fraternity? Would you consider them as important?

Another question to ask, when thinking about just societies, is how to take such vague notions and make them more practical. If a certain country, for instance, has a democratic government, does that mean its citizens are free and equal? How can you ensure equality among all of your citizens when some people are richer or better educated than others? Pierre's government, and those after it, tried to answer these questions, sometimes with success, sometimes with failure.

In 1968, soon after becoming prime minister, Pierre tried to describe what he thought a just society would be. According to Pierre, a just society would be one in which all of our people had the means and motivation to participate. The just society would be one in which personal and political freedoms were more securely ensured than before.

Pierre also explained that a just society would be one in which the rights of minorities were safe from the whims of intolerant majorities. A just society would be one in which regions and groups that have not fully shared in the country's wealth were given a better chance to do so. A just society would be one where problems such as pollution and affordable housing were solved using new knowledge and techniques.

A just society would be one in which Canada's First Nations peoples were encouraged to take on the full rights of citizenship through policies that gave them both greater responsibility for their own future and more meaningful equality of opportunity. A just society would be a united Canada—united because all of its citizens were active in developing a country where equality is guaranteed and individuals can fulfill themselves in the fashion they judge best.

Can you come up with your own ideas of what a just society would be like?

For more information about Pierre's "just society," visit our website at www.jackfruitpress.com.

23

polls, the Liberal party won more than half of the 264 seats in the House of Commons. Clearly Canadians wanted Pierre to lead the country. He was a huge hit!

Two nations, two languages

Right away, Pierre began putting in place the policies that he thought would help Canada become a just society. For example, he knew that Canada had been made by two founding nations, France and England. He believed that both peoples should feel at home in their country. He really wished that all Canadians would be able to speak French and English, like he did. He created the **Official Languages Act**, which recognized English and French as the official languages of all federal institutions in Canada. He believed that French and English Canadians should be able to understand what was being said in their country's Parliament, courts, and federal departments, such as the post office. At the time, all federal government proceedings were conducted in English. Pierre started programs to train people who were working in these places to become bilingual.

Not everyone was crazy about the idea. Some people accused Pierre of forcing French down their throats. Many, especially those living in English communities outside of Quebec, resented having to learn a language they believed they would never have to use. Some people objected to the large sums of money that the government was spending trying to teach adults how to speak French. They thought the money should be spent on other things

The philosopher king?

Long ago, in ancient times, wise men used to say that a philosopher made the best king. Although Pierre was an elected leader, in many ways he behaved like a philosopher king. For example, instead of just running the government like other leaders had done before him, Pierre and his staff met with lots of people to get their ideas about the best way to govern the country. He wanted his government to include the ideas of ordinary Canadians in the decision-making process at all times, not just at election time.

By 1970, the committees and meetings he'd set up had used up a lot of time and money. The people didn't want a lot of discussion anymore; they wanted action. The government went kind of crazy with spending and ran up a **national debt** that skyrocketed from $19 billion to $208 billion. While he was in office, the number of people without jobs soared and there were strikes galore.

Pierre once said, "I entered politics to prove that French Canadians are as good as anyone else; they have no need of a special status, or to be a separate nation."

Pierre genuinely wants a country where everyone gets involved in its politics.

1970

As time goes by, Pierre's government gets bogged down by too much talk, too many studies, too many checks on every decision. The whole country (including Pierre's own cabinet ministers) wants action.

25

The FLQ, an extremist separatist group, has been using bombs to blow up mailboxes in a bid to get media attention. On the morning of October 5, they kidnap a British diplomat and, on October 10, a Quebec politician.

This violent group demands that newspapers and broadcasters announce their political views. They also demand $500,000 in gold and that some of their members be released from prison.

Pierre and the Quebec premier work together, deciding how to respond to the FLQ's demands.

How far am I prepared to go?
Just watch me!

At the height of the crisis, Pierre is interviewed about it. When asked how far he's prepared to go in suspending individual rights to defend national security, Pierre says, "Just watch me!" His popularity plummets in Quebec but skyrockets in the rest of Canada.

Chapter 4

The October Crisis

Around this time, the separatists were becoming more violent in Quebec. Since the early 1960s, some separatists had been using drastic means to get attention, such as blowing up mailboxes. Canadians were nervous. Then came October 5, 1970, and the beginning of what would become known as the October Crisis. On that morning, the British trade commissioner, **James Cross**, was kidnapped from his home in Montreal by **Front de libération du Québec (FLQ)** terrorists. This small group of violent separatists refused to release Cross until the government agreed to their demands, which included publishing and broadcasting their political views supporting separatism, giving them $500,000 in gold, and releasing some of their members from prison.

On October 10, another group of FLQ terrorists kidnapped Quebec's deputy premier, **Pierre Laporte**. The army was called in to help; Quebec's premier, **Robert Bourassa**, believed it would keep citizens safe and might prevent more kidnappings. After troops moved into certain parts of Montreal, Quebec City, and Ottawa, many Canadians were furious. They accused Pierre of trying to take advantage of the situation and crush Quebec separatism.

1970

October 5
British Trade Commissioner James Cross is kidnapped at 8:15 a.m. from his home.

October 10
Pierre Laporte, the deputy premier, is kidnapped around 7 p.m. from his home.

October 12
Soldiers take up positions around Ottawa to protect individuals and sites.

October 13
Pierre makes famous statements to CBC television crews.

October 15
Premier Bourassa requests that the Canadian army be sent to help maintain order.

Within an hour, 1,000 troops arrive; more are deployed over the following days.

October 16
The War Measures Act is imposed at 4 a.m.

Pierre Laporte is killed by his kidnappers.

October 17
The body of Pierre Laporte is found in the trunk of a car.

December 3
James Cross is released and his abductors are flown to Cuba by the Canadian Armed Forces.

Just watch me

Tension mounted. The public worried about the fate of the hostages and wondered who might be next. Some feared large-scale riots and bombings. Pierre consulted with the mayor of Montreal, **Jean Drapeau**, and Premier Bourassa. Fearing that things were getting out of control, they agreed that the **War Measures Act** should be used. This act gave the Quebec Provincial Police, the Montreal city police, the army, and the **RCMP** special powers and took away the usual rights of citizens. For example, the police could search people without having a warrant, and could arrest people without charging them with a crime.

The next day, Pierre was heartbroken to learn that Mr. Laporte had been murdered. At the same time, arrests were occurring. Within 48 hours of the War Measures Act coming into force, almost 250 people in Montreal and some other cities in Quebec were arrested and jailed. By the end of the year, almost 500 were arrested. Most of them were innocent and were eventually let go. Only 62 were ever charged.

The War Measures Act gave the army and the police power to go right into people's houses and take them away—without even charging them first!

The police and army conducted 31,700 such searches, looking for absolutely any signs of involvement with the FLQ.

The mass arrests outraged many people. They thought that Pierre had gone too far. They resented the fact that he was taking away people's rights and freedoms. The leader of the **New Democratic Party (NDP)**, **Tommy Douglas**, agreed. He said Pierre had "used a sledgehammer to crack a peanut." But the prime minister replied, "Peanuts don't make bombs, don't take hostages, and don't assassinate prisoners."

On December 3, Cross was released unharmed after the government agreed that his captors could fly to Cuba. The people who had kidnapped and killed Pierre Laporte were captured on December 28, convicted of their crimes, and sentenced to long prison terms. The FLQ was squashed. The October Crisis was over. The notion of Quebec separating from the rest of Canada, however, still simmered.

Does it make sense to suspend civil rights to protect them?

Governments have a responsibility to safeguard their territories and protect their citizens from harm. In earlier times, this usually meant going to war against invading armies. Now, though, many countries are more concerned about being attacked from within their own borders by terrorists. As fear of such attacks increases, many Canadians feel that the government has a duty to do anything it can to protect them from harm—even if it means suspending people's personal freedoms.

This creates a strange situation: if it's the role of governments to defend the rights of citizens, does it make sense to suspend civil rights in order to protect them? Rights normally taken for granted (like not being arrested without a charge, or not being tortured into making a confession) are now being questioned as authorities try to figure ways of

> There are a lot of bleeding hearts around who just don't like to see people with helmets and guns. All I can say is, go on and bleed, but it is more important to keep law and order.

dealing with alleged terrorists. The only time Canadians faced a challenge like this was during the October Crisis of 1970, when the FLQ kidnapped James Cross and Pierre Laporte. At that time, the Quebec government feared that the

kidnappings might lead to more acts of terrorism. The FLQ claimed it had 100,000 supporters; there was no way of verifying how many people were actually involved.

The army was quickly stationed around government buildings in Ottawa. When questioned about his government's response, Pierre said, "There are a lot of bleeding hearts around who just don't like to see people with helmets and guns. All I can say is, go on and bleed, but it is more important to keep law and order."

When asked how far he might go, Pierre's reply was: "Well, just watch me." Pierre later explained that he believed society must use every means at its disposal to defend itself against powers that threaten its destruction. Canadians massively supported Pierre's hard line. A poll taken that month showed that 88 per cent of Canadians thought the government either did the right thing or should have been even tougher.

Pierre's government responded by invoking the War Measures Act. This allowed police to arrest and imprison people without charge and led to nearly 500 arrests over a couple of months. The army was also called out to patrol the streets and protect places that might be threatened.

But once the crisis was over, facts showed that the threat had been grossly exaggerated and that very few of the people arrested had anything to do with the FLQ. Most Canadians now believe the government overreacted. True, the government's response put an end to the FLQ, but at what cost?

For more information about civil rights, visit our website at www.jackfruitpress.com.

1971

It takes Pierre nearly two years to invite Margaret out on a date. Once he does, an intense courtship follows. The two of them keep their relationship a secret from the whole world.

Their wedding is a complete surprise for everyone. But once Margaret moves into 24 Sussex Drive, the Trudeaus' private lives become the focus of media attention in Canada and around the world. At first, Margaret loves the attention. As times goes by, though, she starts to find public life tiresome.

Chapter 5

Life in the public eye

Shortly after getting elected, new prime ministers usually enjoy a "no hassle" period called "the honeymoon." During this period, the news media, Parliament, and the public go easy on the new PM, giving him a chance to get his bearings, learn the ropes, and generally get accustomed to his new job. Like most PMs, Pierre Trudeau had one of these honeymoons. His, however, lasted a lot longer than usual, and became a bit of a phenomenon. It was called Trudeaumania —and it hit Canada in a big way. Some experts referred to it as a kind of mass hysteria. It was as if all of Canada suddenly fell in love with him. For a while, it seemed as if he could do no wrong. Having Pierre as PM was like having a famous movie star in office. Canadians had never had a celebrity prime minister before. At one point, Pierre was so famous that photos of him were splashed across newspapers, magazines, and television screens in countries around the world.

One of the big factors in Pierre's overwhelming popularity was that he was single when he first came to office. For months after his election as PM, he was surrounded by rumours about women he was dating. All this gossiping was intensified by Pierre's silence on the topic. He had an ace up his sleeve. There was a lady in his life but he was keeping her a secret.

Back in 1970, Pierre had fallen in love with a beautiful girl, **Margaret Sinclair**. She was 22 years old; he was 51. They'd met earlier, in 1967, while both were vacationing on a beach in Tahiti. The two had chatted. Pierre had

1967
Pierre and Margaret Sinclair meet in Tahiti for the first time.

1969
Pierre takes Margaret out on a date.

1971
Pierre and Margaret are married in secret. When the news leaks out, the whole country is abuzz with excitement.

Justin is born on Christmas Day.

1972
Pierre appoints the first female speaker of the **Senate**, Muriel McQueen Fergusson.

1973
A second son, Alexandre, is born on Christmas Day.

1975
A third son, Michel, is born on October 2.

asked Margaret to go deep-sea fishing and they'd arranged to meet at the dock at a certain time. But Margaret stood him up for someone else!

Then almost two years later, in 1969, Pierre, who was now prime minister of Canada, was in British Columbia. Remembering that Margaret lived there, he phoned her. Margaret couldn't believe that the prime minister was calling her for a date! Margaret and Pierre went to a fancy restaurant on top of a mountain where they could look out over Vancouver. It was very romantic. They ate, danced, and had a great time.

Margaret knew that she wanted to see this man again. So she moved to Ottawa and got a job. Imagine moving to another city to be with someone you had only dated once! Margaret got a job as a sociologist with the federal government and settled in. It took her a couple of weeks to get the courage to call Pierre and let him know that she was living there. He seemed pleased and asked her over for a spaghetti dinner. That was the beginning of an intense courtship.

Secret wedding

In the summer of 1970, Margaret and Pierre got engaged. Margaret returned to her parents' home in September, but she and Pierre still managed to see a lot of each other. On March 4, 1971, Margaret and Pierre were married in Vancouver. Pierre almost missed the plane because of a freak snowstorm in Ottawa, but he made it just in the nick of time. The couple had sworn their families to secrecy. Nobody else in Canada knew about the wedding, or even that the couple was engaged! They wed in a simple ceremony at a Catholic church.

The boys of Christmas
Justin and Alexandre (Sacha) Trudeau were both born on Christmas Day.

But it didn't take long for the word to get out. Reporters found them and swarmed the couple's car as they headed to a log cabin up in the mountains. The prime minister had given his staff strict orders not to disturb him unless it was an emergency. The phone rang the next morning at 6:30 a.m. Pierre bolted out of bed. It was Richard Nixon, president of the United States, calling to congratulate him.

Nine months later, on Christmas Day, Justin was born. Canadians were thrilled! It was the first time in 102 years that a child was born to a Canadian prime minister who was in office. Margaret received carloads of presents. Two years later, again on Christmas Day, Alexandre, affectionately called Sacha, popped into the world. Less than two years later, on October 2, 1975, Pierre and Margaret's third son, Michel, was born. Margaret and Pierre's diaper service was kept busy.

The man in the red suit

Although Pierre's job as prime minister kept him incredibly busy, he always found time for his kids. They often went on official visits to different parts of Canada and to foreign countries. One trip was especially memorable. Justin boarded a government plane with his father and they flew north to a scientific military base in Alert, Canada's northernmost point in the Arctic. One freezing cold afternoon, Pierre bundled six-year-old Justin into a Jeep and hustled him out on a top-secret mission.

After driving past some drab grey buildings, they rounded a corner and drove up to a red hut. They all hopped out. Someone boosted Justin up to the window. He rubbed his sleeve on the frosty pane and peeked inside. What did he see? A man dressed in a red suit trimmed with white fur, bent over a work table! "That's when I understood just how powerful and wonderful my father was," Justin recalled later. It's not every child who gets to see Santa at work!

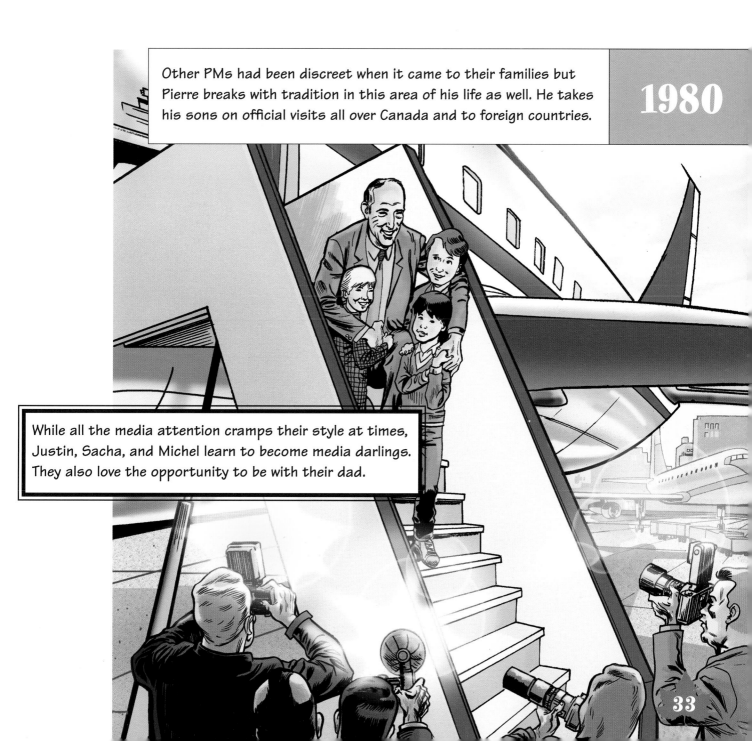

Other PMs had been discreet when it came to their families but Pierre breaks with tradition in this area of his life as well. He takes his sons on official visits all over Canada and to foreign countries.

1980

While all the media attention cramps their style at times, Justin, Sacha, and Michel learn to become media darlings. They also love the opportunity to be with their dad.

1980

As worldwide prices for oil suddenly spike, Pierre's government puts in place a program that freezes the price of Canadian oil. Western Canadians are furious. They believe his government is discriminating against them.

GO BACK TO OTTAWA

NO TO PRICE CONTROL

As Pierre travels across the country, he's greeted with increasing anger and outright hostility. At one point, the train he's travelling in gets pelted with rotten vegetables. Pierre responds by openly mocking the protesters.

Chapter 6

Canada's mood turns sour

Pierre Elliott Trudeau was a powerful man. He was also accused of being an arrogant man who always insisted on doing things his own way—which wasn't necessarily the best way. His attempt to make English **civil servants** bilingual was expensive and mostly unsuccessful. His decision to approve the opening of Mirabel International Airport in Montreal was a financial disaster. At one point, Pierre preached wage cuts and price controls to Canadians and then increased the salaries of **cabinet ministers**—and himself—by 33 per cent. He also approved a special armoured car, in silver-grey, for himself that cost—ready for this?—$80,000!

Arrogant, cocky . . . and yet Pierre was one of the longest standing prime ministers that Canada ever had. After 11 years in office, he lost to the Conservative leader, **Joe Clark**, in 1979. But nine months later, Pierre was back in the saddle, prime minister again!

And then there was the **National Energy Program**, which alienated Western Canada. In 1980, after prices for energy rose dramatically worldwide, Pierre's government put into place the National Energy Program. It kept the price of Canadian oil low, which helped all Canadian businesses and consumers, but it also meant that Alberta lost out on billions of dollars in income because Alberta was producing most of Canada's oil. Western Canadians were furious with Pierre. They believed the federal government was discriminating against them.

1975
The Liberal party implements wage and price controls.

Mirabel airport, Montreal's international airport, opens.

1976
The summer Olympics are held in Montreal.

1977
Pierre and Margaret separate.

1979
Pierre's Liberals lose the election to the Conservatives, led by Joe Clark.

1980
Pierre is re-elected as PM.

The National Energy Program is introduced; this alienates Albertans.

Quebec holds a referendum on the question of separation.
The *Non* vote wins.

1982
The Canadian Constitution is patriated on April 17. It is updated to include the Charter of Rights and Freedoms.

1983-84
Pierre travels to many countries on both sides of the Cold War to convince nuclear powers to reduce their arsenals.

1984
Jeanne Sauvé becomes the first female governor general.

Pierre wins the Albert Einstein Peace Foundation's annual prize.

Pierre announces his retirement from politics, February 29.

John Turner becomes PM.

Will it stay or will it go now?

During his last term of office, from 1980 to 1984, Pierre accomplished three important things. With **Jean Chrétien** as co-chair of the *Non* forces, he helped to prevent Quebec from separating from Canada. The Quebec government believed that Quebecers would be better off and have a stronger identity if Quebec were a separate country. In 1980, it called a referendum. Quebecers were asked to answer one question: Did they want to be independent yet still "associate" with the rest of Canada?

Pierre was furious. He thought this was a trick question and that the Quebec government was trying to make it easier for the people to vote *Oui*. The question made them think they could answer yes and still remain part of Canada. People who wanted Quebec to separate, and people who did not want Quebec to separate completely, could all vote Oui.

Pierre strongly believed that Quebec could not be independent and still be part of Canada. He argued that a separate Quebec would lose all bargaining power, and that the other provinces might say Quebec could have independence but not association with the rest of Canada. He implored Quebecers to vote Non. He said that if they did, the government would not ignore their concerns. It would "immediately take action to renew the constitution."

It was not an easy battle. People were divided on the question. But on May 20, 1980, the results came in. Non: 59.6 per cent. Oui: 40.4 per cent.

Canadians breathed a sigh of relief. Quebec would remain part of Canada.

A grown-up Canada

Pierre also fought for Canada's right to control its own constitution. Canada's constitution is the supreme law of Canada. It sets out the main rules of how the country will be run (for example, how often there will be a federal election). Until that time, many changes to Canada's constitution had to be made by the British parliament.

Canada already had the **Bill of Rights**, which guaranteed Canadians some basic liberties, such as the right to be presumed innocent until proven guilty. But Pierre believed it needed to be improved and updated, so he created a new bill called the **Charter of Rights and Freedoms**. He strongly believed it needed to be included as part of the constitution; this would guarantee that Canadians' rights and freedoms could never be taken away.

Getting agreement on these constitutional issues was much harder than Pierre had predicted. Eight provincial premiers disagreed with him. They believed the constitution would give the federal government too much decision-making power. They held out for more power for their own

Petro-Canada was created in 1975.

At that time, Canada's petroleum industry was mostly controlled by foreign companies.

The main purpose of Petro-Can was to develop and protect Canadian interests in the oil and gas industry.

What's all this fuss about our constitution?

The Canadian Constitution is a living thing. It may be hard to imagine what most people think of as a dusty old document as being alive, but it is—it changes and grows. Think of the constitution as a rule book, like the rules of hockey. Hockey's rules have changed over time; in Canada, the rules change to meet the evolving needs of its citizens.

In 1867, the British North America (BNA) Act, a law enacted by the British parliament, created a federation out of the provinces of Canada (later called Ontario and Quebec), New Brunswick, and Nova Scotia. The power of governing the country was distributed over two levels of government, federal and provincial. The federal government's powers concerned matters of national interest, such as the armed forces, the postal system, and the dollar. The provinces were to control matters of local interest such as municipalities, education, and hospitals.

In 1926, Great Britain decided to let Canada and the other dominions be autonomous. Canada became equal in status to Great Britain. The days were over when the British parliament could tell Canada to fight in a war that Great Britain had joined. In 1931, the Statute of Westminster made it official.

The constitution had to remain in Britain until Canada's federal and provincial governments agreed on how to make changes to it. They needed an "**amending formula.**" The question was: how many people or provinces must agree to a change for it to be considered lawful? In 1949, the BNA act was changed to let the federal government make changes to it for all matters except those that concern the provinces. As the years went on, attempts to reach an agreement with the provinces on an amending formula ended in failure. The British parliament continued to make changes to the constitution when requested by Canada.

It was Pierre Trudeau who championed the final push to get an agreement with the provinces and bring the constitution home. He started working on it in 1968 while he was justice minister in Lester B. Pearson's government. He broadened the scope of the federal/provincial negotiations to include adding the Charter of Rights and Freedoms into the constitution as a replacement for John Diefenbaker's Bill of Rights.

Finally, in 1982, after many negotiations, the provinces (except for Quebec) and the federal government agreed to a complicated amending formula. And so the constitution was brought home, or "patriated"—a word created especially for this process. The BNA act's name was changed to the Constitution Act, 1867. The newer document, signed by Pierre and Queen Elizabeth II on April 17, 1982, was the Constitution Act, 1982. Both of these are part of Canada's constitution, along with other documents and unwritten, less formal agreements, or conventions.

Quebec has still not accepted the amending formula and has not signed the constitution, though it is bound by it. More attempts to make changes that would be acceptable to Quebec have so far failed.

For more information about Canada's constitution, visit our website at www.jackfruitpress.com.

When Pierre became PM, he made sweeping changes to Canada's role as international peacekeepers.

He halved the size of Canada's armed forces and reduced the number of troops in Europe that had been there since World War II.

These decisions certainly did not go over well with Canada's allies, the United States and Europe.

The defence of Canada from forces outside, and separatists inside, the country became the military's top priority.

provincial governments. Eventually, after many meetings and some compromising, all the premiers reached agreement—all except for one. This was **René Lévesque**, premier of Quebec. While Pierre believed that Quebec's culture and language would be protected by the constitution, Lévesque believed that the constitution didn't make it clear that Quebec was a **distinct society**.

Nevertheless, on April 17, 1982, Queen Elizabeth II signed the legal documents that gave Canada power to change its own constitution. It was a red-letter day for Canadians.

Working toward peace

Pierre's third important undertaking was his struggle to bring peace between the superpowers. There had been tension between the United States and the Soviet Union for decades, and both powers had **nuclear weapons**. The possibility of nuclear war scared Pierre. He had protested in demonstrations against nuclear war when he was a student. He had written about the horror of nuclear war in *Cité Libre*. On his travels, he had seen first-hand the devastation that had taken place in **Hiroshima**. He believed that a nuclear war could not be won, and therefore must never be fought.

Hoping he could make a difference and help move the world closer to peace, he visited leaders in Western Europe, India, China, the United States, East Germany, Romania, Czechoslovakia, and the Soviet Union, and talked to them about disarmament. Many people ridiculed his peace initiative. They poked fun at him, the leader of a country with such a small military, for giving advice to superpowers like the United States and the Soviet Union.

In spite of this criticism, Pierre believed that he played some role in getting people to think peace instead of war. He was proud that Canada did what it could "to lift the shadow of war." While Pierre did not directly cause any change in their attitudes, leaders of these powerful countries started to consult and communicate with each other shortly after his visits. Many countries began to "talk peace." In 1985, when the new leader of the Soviet Union, Mikhail Gorbachev, and the president of the United States, Ronald Reagan, met at the **Geneva Summit**, they discussed some of the important issues Pierre had discussed with them. They agreed with his basic belief that if there was nuclear war, the results would be horrific and there would be no winners. They agreed that countries should not be setting themselves up to fight with nuclear weapons.

A life-changing walk in the snow

At the end of his term in 1984, Pierre had to make a most important decision. Should he go on or retire? Seven years earlier, Margaret and Pierre had separated when their marriage fell apart. Although Margaret visited the children often, Pierre was the one who raised them. It was not easy being a single father and the prime minister of Canada. But Pierre had proven that he could do a pretty good job of both!

On the night of February 28, 1984, in Ottawa, he took a long walk in the snow and thought hard about his situation. He knew he wanted to spend more time with his boys, wanted them to have a more ordinary life as teens living in Montreal than they'd had as the prime minister's children. He had completed what he'd entered politics to do, and had done his best; there wasn't much more to give. He thought it was time for somebody else to take over. His decision was released the next day, February 29 (it was a leap year).

Believing that a nuclear war cannot be won and therefore must never be fought, Pierre does what he can to ease the tension between the United States and the Soviet Union, which both have nuclear weapons.

1983-84

Hoping he can help move the world closer to peace, Pierre visits leaders in Western Europe, India, China, the United States, East Germany, Romania, Czechoslovakia, and the Soviet Union and talks to them about disarmament. Many people ridicule Pierre's peace initiative. They poke fun at him, the leader of such a small country, for daring to give advice to superpowers like the United States and the Soviet Union.

1990s

After retiring from politics, Pierre returns to Montreal. He and his three sons move into a newly renovated home. The boys love having their father to themselves.

Pierre and his boys begin travelling a lot together. One summer, they rent a car and drive all over England, Ireland, and Scotland. Another year, they go to China and tour by foot, by train, and by bike.

Chapter 7
Still a lot
to offer

1984
Pierre moves back to Montreal with his sons. He joins the Montreal law firm Heenan Blaikie.

1985
Pierre becomes a Companion of the Order of Canada.

1987
Pierre speaks out against the Meech Lake Accord. The accord is not accepted by every provincial government.

1991
Pierre's daughter, Sarah Coyne, is born.

1992
Pierre speaks out against the Charlottetown Accord. It is rejected in a national referendum.

1993
Kim Campbell becomes Canada's first female PM when Brian Mulroney resigns.

1998
Pierre's youngest son, Michel, dies in a skiing accident.

The Supreme Court rules that Quebec cannot legally separate from Canada without the approval of the federal government.

2000
Pierre dies on September 28.

After Pierre retired, he moved to a house that he'd bought in 1979. It was in Montreal, the former home of a famous Canadian architect and a perfect example of art deco, which was a design style that was popular in the 1920s and 1930s. When Pierre bought the house it was run down, but he hired people to restore it. People called Pierre's newly renovated home everything from a tomb to a museum, but when the kids moved there with their dad in 1984, they loved it.

And they especially loved having their father to themselves. The family began travelling a lot together. One summer, they rented a car and drove all over England, Ireland, and Scotland. Another year, they went to China and toured by foot, by train, and by bike.

In 1984, Pierre joined the Montreal law firm of Heenan Blaikie as an adviser. He worked there when the children were in school. His job seemed pretty simple to him: if any senior lawyers in the firm wanted to talk about an issue or case, they came to him and he gave them good advice. With his experience, he had lots to offer. He enjoyed not having the huge pressures or responsibilities that he had coped with in the days when he was prime minister!

Back in the spotlight

After his retirement, Pierre remained involved in international affairs and often visited foreign leaders. However, he hardly ever spoke to the press or gave public speeches—that is, unless he thought the government of Canada was heading in the wrong direction. This happened on two important occasions. In 1987, there was a meeting at Meech Lake, Quebec, between Prime Minister **Brian Mulroney** and the provincial premiers. Thanks to Trudeau, Canadians were now able to make changes to their own constitution. Quebec was demanding the changes it believed Trudeau had promised after the 1980 referendum. It wanted to be recognized in the constitution as a distinct society with distinct powers. The other provinces were also demanding more powers.

Pierre couldn't sit still. He spoke out strongly against the **Meech Lake Accord**. He believed that Quebec's language, culture, and laws were already well-protected within the constitution, and he didn't think it was fair to give one province special privileges as a distinct society. He also believed that giving more powers to the provinces would weaken the federal government—and Canada.

When it came time for the premiers to officially accept the accord, some of them refused to sign. Others could not sign because they couldn't get it passed through their provincial legislatures. The deal fell through.

But the issues didn't go away. In August 1992, the premiers met in Charlottetown, PEI, to discuss the same concerns—and more. This time, over 60 issues were on the table, including, again, Quebec as a distinct society. Again Pierre arrived on the scene, again against the agreement, which this time was called the **Charlottetown Accord**. He met with the Senate and he talked to many people and groups, trying to persuade them of his view.

He was relieved when, on October 26, 1992, the Canadian people voted against accepting the new changes to the constitution.

Pierre's retirement for the most part was a happy one. It included becoming a **Companion of the Order of Canada** in 1985 and the birth of a new child in 1991, a daughter named Sarah Coyne. But it also brought tragedy. Pierre's youngest son, Michel, died in an avalanche while on a ski trip in British Columbia in 1998. This was a terrible blow—more than Pierre could bear.

Two years later, on September 28, 2000, after suffering from Parkinson's disease and prostate cancer, Pierre died at home with Margaret, Justin, and Sacha by his side.

Canadians from coast to coast mourned his death. The great leader's coffin was placed in the Hall of Honour on Parliament Hill. For two days, over 50,000 people lined up to say their last farewell. They remembered Pierre

Pierre's government gave a lot of power to Canada's provinces, but he personally believed that Canada was much more than just the sum of its parts.

When talking about Canada, he said, "It is not a nation merely because the provinces permit it to be, it is a nation because the Canadian people want it to be."

as an inspiration and a visionary. Then Pierre's body was taken by train to Montreal for a state funeral. The train slowed down as it passed through towns and villages. All along the way people cheered, waved, and wept.

Unable to sit still, Pierre speaks out strongly against the Charlottetown Accord. Pierre is convinced that giving more powers to the provinces will weaken Confederation.

1992

FONY

Favouring one province over others will weaken Canada.

A frustrated Prime Minister Mulroney watches as Pierre takes his case directly to the Senate and his address is televised across the country.

Pierre Elliott Trudeau:

> *"I learned that you win some confrontations just by acting confident."*
>
> *Pierre Elliott Trudeau at the age of 15*

Pierre Trudeau truly was a prankster. He loved to trick people into reacting to his antics. And he certainly enjoyed poking fun at authority or institutions whenever he thought they needed to be taken down a notch. But he was also a man of action, courage, and boldness. He never flinched from making tough decisions, especially when it came to protecting Canada from breaking up or fighting for his dream of a just society.

Those who were annoyed with Pierre thought he was too aloof. They felt that he didn't care about day-to-day matters like the cost of living. They were angered that all he seemed to be passionate about was what Canada would be like in the future.

Most politicians don't work that way. They're usually very good at sensing the people's wishes and giving them what they want. That's often the key to getting elected and staying in power. But Pierre never much cared for power. What he cared about was what Canada would be like 20 or even 30 years in the future: the Canada we now live in.

Thanks to Pierre and his focus on justice, we now live in a more compassionate society. Because of him, Canada's constitution now rests in Ottawa with its own Charter of Rights and Freedoms. Pierre's accomplishments also include youth projects; the defeat of the 1980 Quebec referendum; agreements extending the powers of the provinces and giving them more money and responsibility; and changes to the criminal codes that protect the rights of every person, regardless of race, religion, gender, or sexual orientation. All of these projects, initiated during Pierre's time in office, have an effect on our lives today.

Is it time for the Queen to ma

Dare to imagine a better future

Of course, a big piece of Pierre's legacy is not found in new laws, pirouettes behind the Queen's back, or government programs. His legacy is in the hearts and minds of Canadians. Pierre helped develop a new vision for individuals and for Canada. When his cabinet was drafting the Charter of Rights and Freedoms, they got so involved in the wording, so excited by the dream, that Pierre had to rein in their enthusiasm to get the draft finished.

Like many other great men, Pierre himself was a mystery and what he did seemed almost opposite to what he said. For example, he expected his ministers to manage without him but often undermined their authority. Although he seemed to encourage debate, he had no patience for people who did not argue as well as he did. And what about the War Measures Act? In his youth, he fought against Quebec Premier Duplessis' abuse of power, but then as prime minister allowed almost 500 Quebecers to be arrested and put in jail, even though most of them weren't even charged with committing a crime!

ay for our most famous PM?

At his father's funeral, Justin Trudeau told a touching story that gave us a glimpse of Pierre's character. Eight-year-old Justin was eating with his father at the parliamentary restaurant. He told Pierre a joke about a man seated nearby, thinking that Pierre would laugh along with him since the man was one of Pierre's political rivals. But Pierre said sternly, "Justin, never attack the individual. One can be in total disagreement with someone without denigrating him as a consequence." He then took his son over to the man's table, where they had a friendly chat. Justin learned from his father that it's possible to disagree with an individual but still hold that person in high regard. At the funeral, Justin concluded, "We must have true and deep respect for every human being, regardless of his beliefs, his origins, and his values. That is what my father demanded of his sons, and that is what he demanded of our country."

Timeline: The life and times of Pierre Elliott Trudeau

YEAR	PIERRE'S LIFE	EVENTS IN CANADA AND THE WORLD
1919	Joseph Phillipe Pierre Yves Elliott is born on October 18.	The Winnipeg General Strike occurs from May 15 to June 26. World War I ends.
1920		Arthur Meighen becomes the ninth prime minister of Canada (1920–1921). Women become eligible to sit in the House of Commons. The Progressive party forms.
1921		William Lyon Mackenzie King becomes the 10th prime minister of Canada (1921–1926) and secretary of state for external affairs. Agnes Macphail is the first woman elected to Parliament.
1922		White women are allowed to vote in Prince Edward Island.
1925	Pierre begins school at the Académie Querbes in Montreal.	
1926		Arthur Meighen begins his second term as the 9th prime minister (June 29–September 25, 1926). William Lyon Mackenzie King begins serving his second term as the 10th prime minister on September 25 (1926–1930).
1929		The Judicial Committee of the Privy Council declares women to be legally "persons." The Wall Street stock market crashes, starting the 10-year-long Great Depression.
1930		Richard Bedford Bennett becomes the 11th prime minister of Canada (1930–1935). Cairine Wilson is the first female appointed a senator.
1931	Pierre's father sells his chain of service stations for $1,400,000. He begins at the Jesuit college Jean-de-Brébeuf.	The Statute of Westminster gives Canada the power to change its own constitution, even though it must still take place in the British parliament.
1932		The Co-operative Commonwealth Federation (CCF) party is founded in Calgary.
1933	Pierre travels to Europe for two months with his family.	Adolf Hitler is appointed chancellor of Germany.
1935	Pierre's father dies.	William Lyon Mackenzie King begins his third term as prime minister of Canada (1935–1948). Tommy Douglas wins a seat in the House of Commons in the first election for the Co-operative Commonwealth Federation (CCF) party.
1936		The Canadian Broadcasting Corporation (CBC) is created.
1938		The German army marches into Austria and annexes it to Germany.
1939		Canada declares war on Germany on September 10. World War II begins on September 3 when Britain declares war on Germany (1939–1945).
1940	Pierre begins law school at the University of Montreal.	White women are given the right to vote in Quebec. Canada declares war on Italy on June 10. Germany invades Holland, Belgium, Luxembourg, and France.
1941		Canada, Great Britain, and the United States declare war on Japan.

More on the life and times of Pierre Elliott Trudeau

YEAR	PIERRE'S LIFE	EVENTS IN CANADA AND THE WORLD
1942		The Progressive and Conservative parties unite to become the Progressive Conservative (PC) party. Canada and the United States force citizens of Japanese descent to move inland, away from the west coast.
1943	Pierre graduates from the University of Montreal's law school, then articles for a year.	Canadian troops invade Sicily, Italy. The Alaska Highway is completed.
1944	He enrolls at Boston's Harvard University to study political science and economics.	Ottawa imposes limited conscription for overseas service. Allies land in Normandy, France on D-Day, June 6.
1945	Pierre hitchhikes across Mexico.	The family allowance program (baby bonus) begins. Germany surrenders on May 8. The United States drops two atomic bombs on Japan. Japan surrenders on September 2. The Cold War begins (1945–1990).
1946	Pierre enrolls at both the École libre des sciences politiques and the law faculty of the Sorbonne in Paris.	The first meeting of the United Nations General Assembly takes place in London, England.
1947	Pierre studies for a year at the London School of Economics in Great Britain.	The Canadian Citizenship Act is implemented. India and Pakistan gain independence from Great Britain.
1948	Pierre begins a year-long back-pack adventure from Paris to China.	Louis St. Laurent becomes the 12th prime minister of Canada (1948–1957). South Africa introduces apartheid.
1949		Newfoundland joins Canada.
1950	Pierre begins work at the Privy Council Office in Ottawa. He founds the political magazine *Cité Libre*.	Former prime minister William Lyon Mackenzie King dies. The Korean War begins (1950–53): North Korea invades South Korea. When the fighting ends, the two countries remain divided and officially still at war. No peace agreement has been reached.
1951	He leaves his job in Ottawa to devote his attention to *Cité Libre*.	The first colour television broadcast takes place in five US cities.
1952		The CBC begins TV broadcasts in French and English.
1953		Fidel Castro begins a revolution in Cuba.
1956	Pierre becomes the first vice-president of Le Rassemblement, an organization of opponents of Premier Maurice Duplessis.	The Suez War takes place: Great Britain and France attack Egypt to maintain international control of the Suez Canal.
1957		John Diefenbaker becomes the 13th prime minister of Canada (1957–1963). Ellen Fairclough is appointed Canada's first female cabinet minister.
1959		Fidel Castro becomes president and dictator of Cuba.
1960	Pierre travels to China with Jacques Hébert.	First Nations people are granted the right to vote. The Canadian Bill of Rights is passed.

Still more on the life and times of Pierre Elliott Trudeau

YEAR	PIERRE'S LIFE	EVENTS IN CANADA AND THE WORLD
1961	Pierre becomes an associate professor of law at the University of Montreal.	The CCF party changes its name to the New Democratic Party. The Berlin Wall is built.
1963		Lester B. Pearson becomes the 14th prime minister (1963–1968). The Royal Commission on Bilingualism and Biculturalism begins.
1965	Pierre runs for the Liberal party and wins a seat in the House of Commons.	Lester B. Pearson wins his second term as prime minister. The Maple Leaf flag is adopted. The Canada Pension Plan is established.
1966	Pierre becomes Prime Minister Lester B. Pearson's parliamentary secretary.	Universal medical care is granted. The CBC begins colour television broadcasts. Indira Gandhi becomes prime minister of India.
1967	Pierre meets his future wife, Margaret Sinclair, while on vacation in Tahiti. He's appointed justice minister.	Canada celebrates the 100th anniversary of Confederation. The World Exposition takes place in Montreal. French president Charles de Gaulle visits Montreal and exclaims *Vive le Québec libre* ("Long live free Quebec").
1968	Pierre Elliott Trudeau becomes the 15th prime minister of Canada (1968–1979).	Lincoln MacCauley Alexander becomes the first black MP. René Lévesque founds the separatist Parti Québécois. US civil rights leader Martin Luther King is assassinated.
1969		Parliament and federal institutions are made officially bilingual when the Official Languages Act becomes law. New Brunswick becomes first province to be officially bilingual.
1970		Front de libération du Québec (FLQ) terrorists kidnap two political officials. The War Measures Act is passed, suspending civil liberties.
1971	Pierre secretly marries Margaret Sinclair.	India invades Pakistan.
1972	Pierre begins his second term as prime minister of a minority government. His first son, Justin, in born.	Muriel McQueen Fergusson is appointed the first female speaker of the Senate.
1973	Pierre's second son, Alexandre (Sacha), is born.	A military coup in Chile replaces President Allende with Augusto Pinochet.
1974	Pierre begins his third term as prime minister.	US president Nixon resigns due to the Watergate scandal: he was involved in trying to cover up a break-in of the rival Democrat party's headquarters.
1975	Pierre's third son, Michel, is born.	Toronto's CN Tower becomes the world's tallest freestanding structure. Wage and price controls are implemented (1975–1978).
1976		Joseph Clark is elected leader of the PC party. The summer Olympics are held in Montreal. René Lévesque, leader of the Parti Québécois, becomes premier of Quebec.
1977	Pierre and Margaret separate.	Canadian road signs are changed to show distances and speed limits in metric.
1979	Pierre is voted out of the prime minister's office.	Joseph Clark becomes the 16th prime minister of Canada (June 4, 1979–March 2, 1980). War between the Soviet Union and Afghanistan begins (to 1989).

Even more on the life and times of Pierre Elliott Trudeau

YEAR	PIERRE'S LIFE	EVENTS IN CANADA AND THE WORLD
1980	Pierre is elected to his fourth term as prime minister (1980–1984).	The Quebec referendum on sovereignty is held: the *Non* vote wins. Jeanne Sauvé is appointed the first female speaker of the House of Commons. Terry Fox's Marathon of Hope takes place (April 12–September 2). Canada joins an international boycott of the Olympic summer games in Moscow.
1981		The French-language sign law of Quebec comes into effect.
1982	Along with Queen Elizabeth II, Pierre signs the new Canadian Constitution and the Canadian Charter of Rights and Freedoms becomes law.	The first known cases of Acute Immune Deficiency Syndrome (AIDS) are reported in Canada. The Assembly of First Nations is formed. Bertha Wilson is appointed the first female justice of the Supreme Court of Canada. The Falkland War occurs: Argentina invades the British-owned Falkland Islands. The Lebanon War begins: Israeli forces invade southern Lebanon.
1983		Bertha Wilson is appointed Canada's first female Supreme Court justice. Jeanne Sauvé is appointed the first female governor general. The Internet is created.
1984	Pierre and Margaret's divorce is finalized. Pierre retires from politics. He joins a law firm in Montreal as an adviser.	Aboriginal languages are recognized as official languages in the Northwest Territories. John Turner becomes the 17th prime minister of Canada (June 30, 1984–September 17, 1984). Brian Mulroney becomes the 18th prime minister (1984–1993). Marc Garneau becomes the first Canadian to go into outer space.
1985	Pierre is invested as a Companion of the Order of Canada.	Air India Flight 182, from Toronto, is blown up over the Atlantic Ocean killing 329 passengers; 280 Canadians are killed. Amendments are made to the Indian Act to include the right of First Nations peoples to self-government.
1990		Elijah Harper refuses to accept the Meech Lake Accord in the Manitoba legislature: the accord guarantees no rights to First Nations peoples. Manitoba does not accept the accord, which cancels its acceptance into the Canadian Constitution. The Bloc Québécois party forms. East Germany is united with West Germany.
1991	Pierre's daughter, Sarah Coyne, is born.	The Goods and Services Tax (GST) is introduced. Julius Alexander Isaac becomes the first black chief justice. The Soviet Union collapses as countries declare independence.
1992		The Charlottetown Accord is rejected in a referendum.
1993		Kim Campbell becomes the 19th (and first female) prime minister of Canada (June 25, 1993–November 4, 1993). Jean Chrétien becomes the 20th prime minister (1993–2003).
1998	Pierre's youngest son, Michel, dies in an avalanche in British Columbia.	The Supreme Court rules that Quebec cannot legally separate from Canada without the approval of the federal government. Google Inc. is founded.
2000	Pierre dies at home on September 28.	The Reform party is dissolved and replaced with the Canadian Alliance.

Glossary: Words and facts you might want to know

amending formula: the rules on how to make a change to the Canadian Constitution. There are different rules for different kinds of changes. The general rule is that a change must be passed by the House of Commons, the Senate, and at least two-thirds of the provincial legislatures, representing at least 50 per cent of the population.

Bill of Rights: enacted in Canada in 1960. It guaranteed a variety of civil liberties such as the right to life, freedom from torture, freedom from slavery and forced labour, the right to privacy, the right to a fair trial, freedom of speech, freedom of assembly, freedom of the press, freedom of religion, and the right to marry and have a family.

Bourassa, Robert (1933–1996): premier of Quebec (1970–1976, 1986–1994). A lawyer by training, Robert was chosen to be leader of the Quebec Liberal party in 1970. After winning the election that year, he was immediately faced with the October Crisis. Following his first term as premier, he worked on keeping Quebec in Canada during the first Quebec referendum in 1980.

cabinet minister: a member of the legislature (House of Commons or the Senate) who has been invited by the prime minister to head a major government department or ministry of state. The cabinet acts as a unit; any opinion expressed by a minister is that of the whole cabinet.

Canada World Youth: since 1971, an organization that provides international educational programs for Canadian people aged 17 to 29. Participants gain job skills and learn about other cultures by doing volunteer work in communities around the world. It was founded by former senator Jacques Hébert.

Charlottetown Accord: in 1992, a package of constitutional changes proposed by the Canadian federal and provincial governments to meet Quebec's conditions to sign the constitution. A public referendum was held across Canada on October 26, in which it was defeated.

Charter of Rights and Freedoms: part of the Canadian Constitution (the highest laws in the country) that came into effect in 1982. It is meant to protect citizens from the government. It also protects minorities from parliamentary majorities. The Canadian charter covers several fields: fundamental rights, democratic rights, mobility rights, legal rights, equality rights, and language rights. All laws in the country that do not agree with the charter have no power.

Chrétien, Joseph Jacques Jean (1934–): Canada's 20th prime minister (1993–2003). Born in Shawinigan, Quebec, he practised law before running for federal politics in 1963 as a Liberal.

civil servants: people who work for the government. Examples include teachers, trash collectors, mail carriers, and public-library staff.

Clark, Charles Joseph (Joe) (1939–): Canada's 16th prime minister (1979–1980). He was only 39 years old when he led a minor-ity government, making him the youngest prime minister in Canada's history.

Cold War (1945–1990): the struggle between Russia and the Allies (Great Britain, France, the United States, the USSR, and Canada) after World War II. It was called the Cold War because it didn't lead to widespread fighting, or a "hot" war. Each side accused the other of wanting to rule the world.

Companion of the Order of Canada: the highest degree of the Order of Canada, which recognizes a lifetime of outstanding achievement, dedication to the community, and service to the country. There are 15 appointments of this award per year.

constitution: the highest set of laws in a country. Just like you have rules in your home to help take care of your property, relationships, and personal well-being, a constitution is a set of laws or rules that lays out how a government must take care of its people and the rights these people can expect their government to protect. Most countries have written constitutions that set out the basic laws of their state.

criminal code: the set of government laws that outlines Canada's criminal offences and the maximum and minimum punishments that courts can impose upon offenders when they commit those crimes. It was first enacted in 1892.

Cross, James Richard (1921–): British diplomat in Canada who was kidnapped in Montreal by the Front de libération du Québec (FLQ) during the October Crisis of

More words and facts you might want to know

October 1970. He was released in exchange for safe passage for his kidnappers to Cuba.

distinct society: (in French, *la société distincte*), a term used to describe the uniqueness of Quebec within Canada.

Douglas, Thomas Clement (Tommy) (1904–1986): premier of Saskatchewan (1944–1961), first leader of the federal New Democratic Party (NDP) (1961–1971). He created the socialist Co-operative Commonwealth Federation (CCF) party, which joined with organized labour to create the NDP.

Drapeau, Jean (1916–1999): mayor of Montreal (1954–1957, 1960–1986). During his 29 years as mayor, he hosted the 1967 World Exposition and the 1976 Summer Olympic Games. He resigned from the position after suffering a stroke.

Duplessis, Maurice LeNoblet (1890–1959): lawyer, premier of Quebec (1936–1939, 1944–1959), and leader of the now-defunct Union Nationale party. He was a highly controversial politician and was seen as anti-union and against people having basic rights and freedoms. However, under his leadership, the Quebec government balanced its books 15 years in a row even as it launched huge public works, including highway and hydroelectric projects, and university, school, and hospital construction.

Elliott Trudeau, Grace (1891–1973): mother of Pierre Elliott Trudeau and wife of Charles Émile Trudeau. She was of French and Scottish descent and spoke both French and English. She also had a daughter, Pierre's older sister Suzette, and another son, Pierre's younger brother, Charles.

Front de libération du Québec (FLQ): founded in 1963, a separatist group in Quebec that used terrorism to promote Quebec's independence from Canada. Until 1970, the group was involved in many bombings in Montreal. In the fall of 1970, the FLQ kidnapped Pierre Laporte, a provincial politician, and James Cross, a British trade commissioner.

Geneva Summit (1985): a two-day international meeting held in Geneva, Switzerland, to begin easing the tension due to the Cold War between the United States and the Soviet Union. Ronald Reagan and Mikhail Gorbachev met for the first of their five summits to discuss eliminating nuclear and chemical weapons and a new commitment to human rights.

governor general: the representative of the king or queen in Canada who provides the royal assent necessary for all laws passed by Parliament. The governor general is a figurehead who performs symbolic, formal, ceremonial, and cultural duties, and whose job is to encourage Canadian excellence, identity, unity, and leadership. Governors general are Canadian citizens appointed for terms of approximately five years. During their term, they live and work in the official residence of Rideau Hall in Ottawa.

Hébert, Jacques (1923–): born in Montreal, a writer, publisher, and senator (1983–1998). With his previous newspaper experience, he helped expand the reach and influence of Trudeau and

Pelletier's *Cité Libre*. A champion of democracy and youth in Canada, he was a founding member of the Quebec Civil Liberties Union and founder of both Katimavik and Canada World Youth.

Hiroshima: in Japan, the first city in history to be subjected to nuclear warfare. During World War II, on August 6, 1945, a nuclear weapon was dropped by a US air force bomber killing an estimated 80,000 civilians immediately and heavily damaging the city. Many more died in the following years from the effects of nuclear radiation. Three days later, Nagasaki was bombed, also by a nuclear weapon. Japan surrendered on August 15, thus ending the war.

House of Commons: the lower house of Parliament. It consists of a speaker, the prime minister and his cabinet, members of the governing party, members of the opposition parties, and sometimes a few independent members (elected members who do not belong to an official party). The members of the House (called members of Parliament or MPs) are elected in constituency elections or by-elections by the Canadian people. The House (often incorrectly referred to as Parliament) is important because it is where all new laws start.

Jesuits: or the Society of Jesus; one of the largest religious orders in the Roman Catholic Church. It was founded in 1540 by St. Ignatius Loyola. Today, Jesuits number over 20,000 all over the world. Jesuit priests and brothers focus on education, primarily at colleges and universities, as well as missionary work.

More words and facts you might want to know

Katimavik: founded in 1977 by retired senator Jacques Hébert, a Canadian national youth volunteer-service program. For nine months, young people aged 17 to 21 live in groups of 11 in different communities throughout the country. They work on community projects in addition to having structured learning activities.

Laporte, Pierre (1921–1970): provincial cabinet minister of the Quebec Liberal party (1962–1966, 1970). He was kidnapped and murdered by the FLQ during the October Crisis.

Lesage, Jean (1912–1980): premier of Quebec (1960–1966). Born in Montreal, he began politics in the federal Parliament as a member of the Liberal party (1945–1958). In 1958, Lesage became leader of the Quebec Liberal party. In the provincial election of 1960, the Liberals swept into office. The next six years brought many changes to Quebec society, so much so that this time became known as the Quiet Revolution.

Lévesque, René (1922–1987): journalist and premier of Quebec (1976–1985). A former Liberal member of the Quebec National Assembly, he founded the Parti Québécois in 1968 because he disagreed with the Liberal party's stand on how Quebec fit into Canada. His government's Bill 101 made French the official language of Quebec. In 1980, he was defeated in a referendum on whether Quebec should split from Canada while maintaining a sovereignty association with it.

Liberal Party of Canada: political party that adopted its name after Confederation in 1867. It was formed from the union of the pre-Confederation Reform party (of what is now Ontario) and le Parti rouge (in what is now Quebec).

Marchand, Jean (1918–1988): union leader and politician. Born in Champlain, Quebec, he became a union organizer in 1944. He disagreed with Premier Maurice Duplessis' policies and worked to see that his party was defeated in the 1960 election. As president of the Confederation of National Trade Unions, he worked closely with the new government of Jean Lesage to bring in reforms to help the workers. In 1965, Jean and his old friends Pierre Trudeau and Gérard Pelletier won seats in the House of Commons and went to Ottawa as the "Three Wise Men" from Quebec.

Meech Lake Accord: in 1987, a set of proposed changes to the Canadian Constitution. They were designed and negotiated by Prime Minister Brian Mulroney and the provincial premiers to meet Quebec's conditions for signing the constitution, which had been patriated from Great Britain in 1982. Although the accord was accepted by all premiers and the prime minister at the meetings that were held at Meech Lake in Quebec, it was not approved by all provincial legislatures. It was therefore never enacted.

member of Parliament (MP): politician who is elected to sit in the House of Commons. During a general election, the country is divided up into ridings (or constituencies). The voters in each riding elect one candidate to represent them in the government as their MP.

Mulroney, Martin Brian (1939–): 18th prime minister of Canada (1984–1993). Brian was born in Quebec to Irish immigrants, and trained as a lawyer. Without ever having run for office, Brian became leader of the Progressive Conservative party in 1983. In 1984, he led the PC party to win 211 seats, the most in Canadian history.

national debt: the total amount of money that the federal government has borrowed and not paid back in all the years it has been in existence. It includes all the money that it owes to anybody, including its own citizens who have bought government bonds for investment purposes.

New Democratic Party (NDP): founded in 1961, a national political party that was created when the Co-operative Commonwealth Federation (CCF) merged with unions within the Canadian Labour Congress. The CCF wanted to get better results in elections; the unions wanted an official way to become involved in politics. While it has yet to be in power federally, the NDP has formed the governments of Ontario, British Columbia, Yukon, Saskatchewan, and Manitoba.

nuclear weapons: weapons that get their destructive force from the nuclear reactions of nuclear fission and/or fusion. They are much more powerful than conventional explosives, and a single weapon is capable of destroying an entire city.

For more information on the terms listed in this glossary, visit www.jackfruitpress.com

Still more words and facts you might want to know

parliamentary secretary: assistant to a cabinet minister. In the Legislative Assembly of Ontario, they are called "parliamentary assistants."

Pearson, Lester Bowles (1897–1972): Canada's 14th prime minister (1963–1968). He was a man of several careers before he entered politics, including history professor, secretary in the Canadian High Commission during World War II, ambassador to the United States, and deputy minister of external affairs. He received the Nobel Peace Prize in 1957.

Pelletier, Gérard (1919–1997): journalist, federal politician (1965–1975), and friend of Pierre Elliott Trudeau. The trio of Pelletier, Trudeau, and Jean Marchand (known as the "Three Wise Men" in English and *Les trois colombes* [the three doves] in French) were recruited by Prime Minister Lester B. Pearson to combat the growing separatist movement in Quebec.

Privy Council Office: a department of public servants (not elected politicians) who support the prime minister and the cabinet in the operation of the government of Canada. Among other things, this group helps the cabinet and its committees prepare for and conduct meetings.

Progressive Conservative (PC) party: the name of the Conservative Party of Canada following its union with some members of the farm-focused Progressive party in 1942. The Conservative party began in 1854 when politicians from Upper and Lower Canada joined to form a coalition government of the Province of Canada. Sir John A. Macdonald was its first leader. In 2004, the party merged with the Canadian Alliance to become the new Conservative party.

Queen Elizabeth II (1926–): Queen of the United Kingdom, Canada, and her other Realms and Territories, Head of the Commonwealth, Defender of the Faith. She acceded to the throne following her father's death in 1952. She proclaimed Canada's constitution in 1982.

Quiet Revolution (1960–1966): or, *Révolution tranquille*, a time when Quebec experienced much change. The Quebec Liberal party introduced reforms to modernize the province after 24 years under the leadership of the Union Nationale, a party that held on tightly to outdated, old-fashioned values. A new age of open debate took place when every policy was examined.

Royal Canadian Mounted Police (RCMP): the federal police for all of Canada and the largest police force in Canada, with over 20,000 members. The three Canadian territories and eight of the ten provinces use the RCMP as their provincial/territorial police force. Ontario, Quebec, and parts of Newfoundland and Labrador have their own provincial police forces. Many towns and cities across Canada also contract the RCMP to serve as their local police force.

Senate: the upper house of Parliament. Here, senators examine and revise legislation from the House of Commons, the lower house of Parliament, investigate national issues, and represent regional, provincial, and minority interests. The Senate can also introduce its own bills.

Sinclair Trudeau, Margaret (1948–): born in Vancouver, British Columbia, former wife of Pierre Elliott Trudeau. Together they had three sons: Justin, Alexandre (Sacha), and Michel. Margaret and Pierre separated in 1977.

Trudeau, Charles Émile (?–1935): father of Pierre Elliott Trudeau. The son of a farmer, he became a lawyer before going into business. He made his family wealthy when he sold a series of 30 gas stations to Imperial Oil in 1932. He died when Pierre was 15.

24 Sussex Drive: in Ottawa, the official residence of the prime minister of Canada since 1951. The house was built in 1866 by mill owner and member of Parliament Joseph Merrill Currier as a wedding gift to his bride Hannah. He called the home *Gorffwysfa*, a Welsh word meaning "place of peace."

World War II (1939–1945): a conflict that involved almost every part of the world. The main participants were Axis powers—Germany, Italy, and Japan—and the Allies—France, Great Britain (including Canada and Australia), the United States, and the USSR. The war was a continuation of problems left unresolved by World War I. It was the largest war in history and ended with the defeat of the Axis countries.

Index

Is this a great country or what?

We've got the Rockies, the Mounties,
the Prairies, and the Barenaked Ladies.

And how about those Prime Ministers?
In their own way, they're a natural wonder too.
Each one as different as a snowflake...

Some of them made us laugh,
some made us cringe.
Others even made us furious.

Get to know each one.
One at a time.
Warts and all.

JackFruit

www.jackfruitpress.com